Boys in a Box

Carlo Zezza

Why our top college crews are rowed by foreigners,

Why our men won no medals at the Rio Olympics,

And what we can do about it

Boys in a Box - ISBN-13: 978-1541216761
ISBN-10: 1541216768

Copyright 2017 © Carlo Zezza

Any part of this book may be quoted or reproduced without prior permission from the copyright holder; "Boys in a Box' by Carlo Zezza" should be cited as source for extensive quotation.

Preface

In the summer of 2016, at the IRA championship regatta for men, 14 of the 16 men in the varsity crews that finished 1st and 2nd were not Americans. They came from Europe (9), Great Britain (4), and Australia (1).

Ten weeks later, the Rio Olympics marked the first time in over a hundred years that our men failed to earn a rowing medal.

A strong connection exists between the lack of USA-trained oarsmen in American collegiate crews, and our men's Olympic disappointment. Development of our young rowers is boxed in by tradition, inertia, misunderstanding, and conflicting priorities. This book presents facts and figures to document the reasons.

The following pages trace our separation from rowing in the rest of the world, with a glance at Britain's recovery from an Olympic medal drought amid issues similar to ours today. Spending in the USA is compared to other rowing nations, with focus on our huge expenditure for college rowing and its consequent distorting effects on development of our Junior, U23 and Senior teams.

A look at medals earned by male "A" finalists, before the Rio Olympics, shows that many started winning internationally while in their early 20's, when our own athletes are barely out of college, and a review of other countries' 'best practices' shows how kids from overseas get a head start, in international competition and in their competition for seats in our own top varsities.

We have excellent, but too few, programs aimed at competition in the international boat classes, and these are noted as 'dots of light on a dark continent'. Their potential can only be realized if USRowing fulfills its obligation as National Governing Body (NGB). As explained, this obligation requires a competition-driven mission.

Short-term adjustments at the top of our high performance ladder may well be needed, but any initiative will fail if it ignores the fundamental long-term solution, of having our young rowers train and compete in the boats that are raced everywhere else. It is the way to level medal opportunities for big and small college programs.

It is the only way to achieve our potential, for our athletes, for our sport, and for our pride as a rowing nation.

On January 20th, 2017, Row2k reported the resignation of USRowing's CEO, effective April 15th, as well as the resignations of four directors, including the incumbent president and treasurer. As winds of change blow at USRowing, the facts and figures in "Boys in a Box" are ever more relevant.

Contents

Chapter One
History - The Decline and Fall 1

Chapter Two
Money and Priorities 11

Chapter Three
Champions Start Young – Retention and the Will to Win 21

Chapter Four
Best Practices 29

Chapter Five
Dots of Light on a Dark Continent 39

Chapter Six
USRowing's Obligations 45

Chapter Seven
Achieving Our Potential as a Rowing Nation 53

Appendix A - College spending for rowing i
Appendix B - A narrative, October '15 to August '16 iii
Appendix C - Facts, sources, & assumptions x

Chapter One
History - The Decline and Fall

Sweeps and Sculls

The Yale eight won gold in Melbourne in 1956, marking the seventh Olympiad of U.S. college victories (our win in Berlin was the subject of Daniel James Brown's best-seller "The Boys in the Boat"). Our 34-year tradition ended when a German eight took gold in Rome, in 1960. A U.S. eight sponsored by Vesper Boat Club finished 5th. We rebounded in the next Olympics but then, despite brilliant moments like our world record at the Athens Olympics, our men's achievement has dwindled to a goose egg in Rio.

The chart below shows the trend.

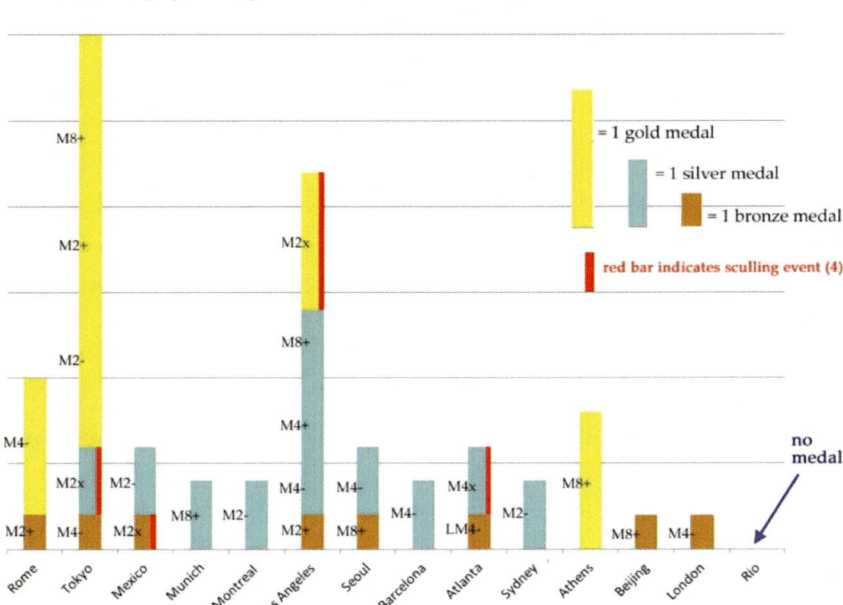

Out of 25 medals won by the USA between 1960 and 2012, 21 were in sweeps, and only 4 in sculling, none recent. The imbalance illustrates our problem.

Like many other outdoor activities, rowing as sport owes its origins and prestige to the British Empire (see Note 1). The oldest rowing race, dating from 1715, is Doggett's Coat & Badge, a sculling competition for young watermen on the Thames. At the upper end of the economic scale, Britain's great 'public' schools established sport as part of a gentleman's education. 'Dry bobs' played cricket or rugby and 'wet bobs' rowed, with sweeps.

To our benefit, American schools took over the British concept of sport in school. We also took over, with less benefit, the idea that schoolboys and collegians row with sweeps. At the end of the 19th century, betting scandals killed interest in the professionals who competed in singles, doubles and pairs, and, by comparison, enhanced the honest virtue of schoolboys and collegians, rowing eights and fours.

To this day, although sweeps and sculls share identical dynamics, most U.S. rowers perceive them as fundamentally different. In Europe and the rest of the non-Anglo Saxon world, no distinction exists. A single word *(aviron, rudern, canottaggio,* etc.), covers all rowing. Rowers are expected to be proficient in both. For them, there is no difference.

Olympic Boat Classes

Rowers are few compared to almost all other sports (Note 3 lists thirty sports by participation, with rowing close to the bottom). Despite rowing's tiny presence in the world at large, rowers at the Olympics are only outnumbered by track & field. The large number of Olympic rowers puts a point on structuring rowing events to achieve overall Olympic goals.

These commendable goals are for broader inclusion and enhanced medal opportunities for smaller countries. Opportunities for small boats have been increased at the expense of big boat sweeps, because a small country can hope for a world-class single, double, or pair, while a competitive eight might be out of reach.

The following chart shows how Olympic boat classes have evolved away from sweeps. 4 of the 8 men's events in Rio were for scullers. The Tokyo Olympics in 2020 will offer 7 men's events, 4 for sculls and 3 for sweeps. In addition to more small boat events, more countries are invited to compete in small boats, while limits on big boat entrants have been reduced.

Along with shrinkage in sweeps classes, only the eight remains as a coxed crew. The coxed pair succumbed as of 1976, and the coxed four in 1996. Of the boats rowed in US collegiate heavyweight competition, only the coxed eight is rowed in the Olympics.

Men's Boat Classes in International Competition 1960 - 2016 + 2020 (expected)

5 sweeps/2 sculls				5 sweeps/3 sculls				4 sweeps/4 sculls						3 sweeps 4 sculls
M8+	M8+	M8+	M8+	M8+	M8+	M8+	M8+	M8+	M8+	M8+	M8+	M8+	M8+	M8+
M4+	M4+	M4+	M4+	M4+	M4+	M4+	M4+	~	~	~	~	~	~	~
M4-	M4-	M4-	M4-	M4-	M4-	M4-	M4-	M4-	M4-	M4-	M4-	M4-	M4-	M4-
M2+	M2+	M2+	M2+	M2+	M2+	M2+	M2+	LM4-	LM4-	LM4-	LM4-	LM4-	LM4-	~
M2-	M2-	M2-	M2-	M2-	M2-	M2-	M2-	M2-	M2-	M2-	M2-	M2-	M2-	M2-
M1x	M1x	M1x	M1x	M1x	M1x	M1x	M1x	M1x	M1x	M1x	M1x	M1x	M1x	M1x
M2x	M2x	M2x	M2x	M2x	M2x	M2x	M2x	M2x	M2x	M2x	M2x	M2x	M2x	M2x
				M4x	M4x	M4x	M4x	M4x	M4x	M4x	M4x	M4x	M4x	M4x
								LM2x	LM2x	LM2x	LM2x	LM2x	LM2x	LM2x
1960	1964	1968	1972	1976	1984 Los Angeles	1988	1992	1996	2000	2004	2008	2012	2016	2020
Rome	Tokyo	Mexico	Munich	Montreal		Seoul	Barcelona	Atlanta	Sydney	Athens	Beijing	London	Rio	Tokyo expected

At the Rio Olympics, the British qualified entries in each of the eight men's events. Our men were able to qualify in five, lacking any sculling entry except the lightweight men's double. From the outset, our medal opportunities were limited.

The Olympic organizers have achieved the goal of expanding medal possibilities to more countries, with medals earned by 21 of the 69 nations present in Rio.

Among the 21 nations that won medals, USA earned gold for the women's eight and silver for the women's single. Women's rowing since 1976 has been the salvation of our rowing reputation, and our magnificent women's eight, along with silver medals in women's singles, won by Michelle Guerette in Beijing, and Gevvie Stone in Rio, have earned our heartfelt thanks.

Increased opportunity for smaller countries has played away from our focus on sweeps, while the gap between winners and losers is getting smaller. Crews that could have earned a bronze medal in 1960 might struggle to get in the "A" final today. Achieving parity is not enough. The following chart shows the narrowing gap between men's "A" finalists at the Olympics.

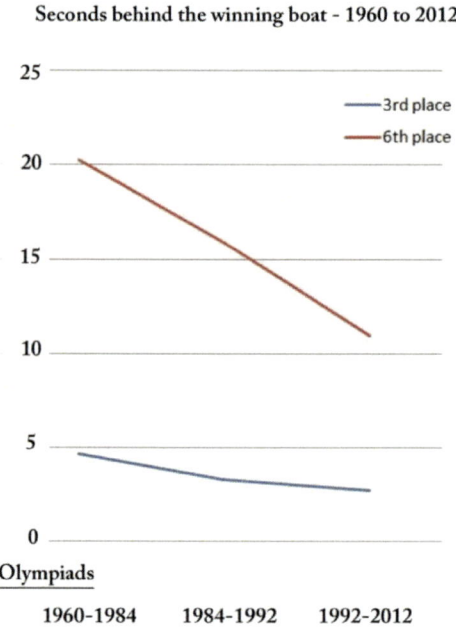

Gold medals for the British eight in Rio and for the German eight in London suggest that skills learned in small boats make more efficient sweeps rowers. In fact, all but one of the 12 sweeps boats that reached the podium in Rio came from a nation that starts beginners in sculling boats; the lone exception was the Australian four that earned a silver medal.

The notion that scullers row better than sweepers, even in sweeps boats, is supported by victories of "Great Eights", rowed by the world's best scullers, over national team eights at the Head of the Charles.

Our colleges' recruitment of overseas rowers to row in eights leads to the same conclusion. Preference for overseas rowers is true not only for men's crews, but also for collegiate women (see Note 2).

Summing up, <u>rowing in the USA has been left behind by the rest of the world</u>. Winning internationally requires rare individuals, ones out of thousands. They can come from anywhere, but odds favor larger pools of gifted well-coached competitors, and local competition in the Olympic classes. Our talent pool of young rowers with waterman skills is disproportionally small, because the great majority of our kids don't start in sculling boats that dominate international competition. And – as described in the following chapter – our most promising talents are too often wasted because of conflicting priorities in collegiate competition.

<u>The British experience - rags to riches</u>

Our men's present disappointment is paralleled in British history, and a look at that history is instructive.

The past four Olympics have seen Britain emerge as the most successful rowing nation. Their success follows a 20-year drought (as shown on the next page) when only one medal was earned in six successive Olympiads. Today, we point to Britain's lottery funding to explain their success. But British lottery funds are awarded to winners, not laggards. Lottery funding was awarded <u>after</u> a resurgence of British rowing; it was not the cause.

In the 70's, Britain's adults reorganized to succeed in international competition. They started their kids in sculling boats. Since the late

1970's, young Brits can only compete in sweeps races after passing their 16th birthday on January 1st. The effect is that most are 17 when they first race with sweeps.

British Olympic Results

Olympic regatta	Gold	Silver	Bronze	Total
2016 Rio	3 (M8+, M4-, W2-)	2 (W8+, W2x)	0	5
2012 London	4 (W2-, W2x, M4-, LW2x)	2 (LM2x, LM4-)	3 (M1x, M2-, M8+)	9
2008 Beijing	2 (M4-, LM2x)	2 (M8+, W4x)	2 (M2x, W2x)	6
2004 Athens	1 (M4-)	2 (W4x, W2-)	1 (W2x)	4
2000 Sydney	2 (M4-, M8+)	1 (W4x)	0	3
1996 Atlanta	1 (M2-)	0	1 (M4-)	2
1992 Barcelona	2 (M2-, M2+)	0	0	2
1988 Seoul	1 (M2-)	0	1 (M2+)	2
1984 Los Angeles	1 (M4+)	0	0	1
1980 Moscow	0	1 (M8+)	2 (M2-, M4-)	3
1976 Montreal	0	2 (M2x, M8+)	0	2
!952-1972	British drought years			
1972 Munich	0	0	0	0
1968 Mexico City	0	0	0	0
1964 Tokyo	0	1 (M4-)	0	1
1960 Rome	0	0	0	0
1956 Melbourne	0	0	0	0
1952 Helsinki	0	0	0	0
1948 London	2 (M2-, M2x)	1 (M8+)	0	3
1936 Berlin	1 (M2x)	1 (M4-)	0	2
1932 Los Angeles	2 (M2-, M4-)	0	0	2
1928 Amsterdam	1 (M4-)	2 (M2-, M8+)	1 (M1x)	4
1924 Paris	2 (M1X, M4-)	0	0	2
1920 Antwerp	0	2 (M1x, M8+)	0	1
1912 Stockholm	2 (M1x, M8+)	2 (M8+, M4+)	0	3
1908 London	4 (M1x, M2-, M4- M8+)	3 (M1x, M2-, M4-	1 (M8+)	8
1904 St Louis		absent		
1900 Paris	0	0	1 (M1X)	1

British youngsters gain waterman skills at an early age. Many of ours never do. ("Waterman" is a compliment for either gender.)

Lottery funding has enabled other positive initiatives, including recruiting (Britain's START program), to identify youngsters with promising genetic and personality gifts, and develop them with a consistent training program on a path defined by country-wide age standards.

Like the USA and unlike Europe, most British rowers begin in schools. Like our schools, dealing with hordes of teens is easier in big boats than in singles and doubles. In Britain, many school kids row in coxed quads and coxed octuples. The following table shows the predominance of sculling for British scholastic rowers.

<u>More British kids race in octuples than in eights!</u>

British National School Regatta - 2012
rowers by boat class

Girls		Boys	
		2-	42
		4-	124
4+	140	4+	324
8+	<u>48</u>	8+	<u>408</u>
	188		898
1x	71	1x	114
2x	206	2x	220
4x	136	4x	184
4x+	276	4x+	456
8x+	<u>136</u>	8x+	<u>400</u>
	825		1374

Some may argue that an octuple or a quad is no better than an eight or a four for teaching. As a matter of opinion, the lighter weight and smaller blade of a sculling oar give better feedback than a sweep. But the main benefit of starting in big sculling boats is a seamless transition into doubles and singles.

Starting youngsters in sculling boats is an example that we should not ignore, as amplified in Chapter Three on Best Practices.

The most important lesson from the British experience is that proactive, caring adults can institute change for the benefit of future competitors. We have many caring adults. We only lack clear goals, leadership, and willingness to change.

Twelve year old boys about to launch in a fleet of coxed quads on the Upper Thames, Maidenhead, England

Notes to Chapter One

Note 1 - Mountain climbing, alpine skiing, croquet, boxing, golf, and racing sailboats around buoys were all British inventions

Note 2 – At the 2015 NCAA championships, only 4 American girls rowed in the 1st & 2nd place varsity eights. 12 came from elsewhere (4 from Australia, 2 each from Britain &Norway, and 1 each from Canada, Germany, New Zealand, and Spain).

Note 3 - The table below lists USA participants in various sports. Numbers are culled from a variety of sources. 44x more people row regularly on indoor rowing machines than on water.

Participants - Selected Sports - various sou ('000)
(not all the same year, or same level of participation)

75,290	Treadmill/Elliptical
51,320	Aerobics
43,560	Stationary Bike
28,000	Running (50x/yr)
24,700	Golf
19,000	Archery
19,000	Running (competitive)
17,900	Tennis
14,000	Skeet & Trap Shooting
12,500	Skiing & Snowboarding
9,910	Tennis (10x/yr)
9,790	Canoeing
4,400	Rowing machine (50x/yr)
3,920	Sailing
3,590	Racqetball
2,800	Stand Up paddling
2,600	Cross country skiing
2,420	Hockey (all)
2,030	Sea kayaking
1,600	Squash
1,600	Bowling (league members)
1,550	White-water kayaking
533	Hockey (registered amateurs)
404	Swimming (USASwimming members)
260	Triathlon (competitive)
178	Figure skating
±100	Rowing
77	Running (marathon entrants)
30	Petanque/Bocce
15	Curling
8	Croquet (competitive)

Chapter Two
Money and Priorities

The following table compares 2015 full-year expenditures by National Governing Bodies (NGBs) for rower talent development in several countries (see Note 1 on funding overseas). The immediate conclusion is that USA's spending <u>at the NGB level</u> is comparable to other countries. (Note 2 describes the origin of the following estimations). Listed alphabetically:

<u>NGB Annual Expense 2015</u>	(US $ '000)	
Australia -	5,600	3/4 competition
Britain	14,500	2/3 competition
Canada	6,000	3/5 competition
Germany	5,500	all competition
Italy	4,400	3/4 competition
New Zealand	3,500	all competition
USA	9,300	1/2 competition

Our NGB, USRowing, is only a small part of the financial story in the USA. The next page provides a top-to-bottom picture of <u>total</u> funding for talent development in the USA, compared to Germany (see Note 3).

The number that jumps off the page is <u>$ 95 million for collegiate rowing in the United States</u>. This <u>dwarfs all other nations, and all other spending within the USA</u>.

($ MM)	USA	Germany
NGB level (international goals)		
National Team	4.0	2.5
U 23 *	0.3	0.3
Junior *	0.7	0.7
USRowing affiliated		
Training Centers	4.0	--
Camps *	2.0	2.0
non-NGB		
Clubs	8.0	15.0
number	(± 25)	(± 260)
total of above	19.0	20.5
Scholastic/Collegiate		
Schools	15.0	--
number	(± 400)	
Collegiate Clubs & non-Title IX Colleges (ACRA)	15.0	--
College Camps	2.0	
Title-IX compliant Colleges	**95.0**	
number	(116)	
total Scholastic/Collegiate	127.0	--
total of above	146.0	20.5

* USA expenditure includes estimated athlete-paid expenses - clubs, camps, travel, etc.

A detailed list of expenditures reported by 116 rowing institutions is shown in Appendix A. (Reports are required to show Title IX compliance. "Title IX" means equal support for men and women.)

A glance at the list shows that top programs spend in the neighborhood of $ 2 million up to $ 3 million annually for rowing.

Collegiate money for all sports comes from many sources. The biggest support for rowing originates from broadcast rights to college football and basketball games. NCAA's broadcast deal for the "March Madness" basketball tournament is an eye-popping 22 BILLION dollars. Football rights are negotiated separately by football-playing conferences, some with their own revenue-producing TV networks. College football and basketball may be "non-profit", but they are a big business, where conference commissioners earn salaries in the millions.

Institutions with basketball and football revenue have corresponding costs, and a corresponding need to sponsor women's sports for Title IX gender balancing.

Non-revenue men's sports are candidates for elimination. Many medium-sized colleges no longer sponsor men's crew, while many more have added women's crew in order to even up their Title IX equation. The result is that only a quarter of collegiate spending for rowing is devoted to men. But even a quarter is substantial - <u>23 million dollars declared for collegiate men,</u> plus a few million more for undeclared student financial aid in Ivy institutions, compares with any other country's entire expense for talent development.

A rich sports environment should provide world-class athletes to represent the USA internationally. Our National Team women have certainly benefited. For men's crew, the opposite has been true. <u>Collegiate rowing sucks away the potential for our men to achieve parity with other nations</u>, because potentially great small boat rowers are lost to rowing sweeps.

Bright teenagers worldwide are keenly attracted by four years of financial aid and a diploma from a world-recognized USA university (see Note 4). Our student-athlete financial aid is a mighty magnet, and <u>colleges compete in sweeps</u>. Our schools and many clubs will never place full emphasis on small boats, unless collegiate financial aid opportunities are tied to competition in the international boat classes. Otherwise, there are too many reasons to row in coxed eights and coxed fours:

... tradition is tied to sweeps

... coaches know sweeps but aren't familiar with sculls (although there is little difference)

... unwanted expense of conversion of fours to quads, purchase of small boats and oars, additional supervision

... inconvenience of scheduling and supervising more boats

... perceived safety concerns with more boats on the water

Our top colleges' preference for overseas rowers is not well publicized. It may be unknown to many aspiring school rowers in the USA. It might promote a desire to row in small boats, if our school coaches and young rowers understood that they are now locked into a losing system. The following graphic illustrates why our top college crews are rowed by foreigners.

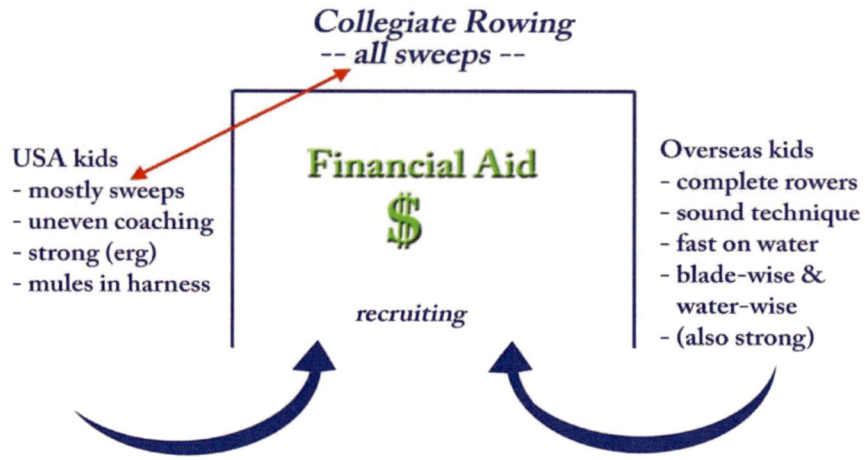

Why half of top College crews are from overseas

The preceding should not suggest that promising US scholastic rowers cannot find student-athlete financial aid. In fact, only the top varsities with the biggest budgets have a preponderance of rowers from overseas. A few notches down from the top, seats and financial aid are available to home-grown kids with strong erg scores. The following is an estimation of participation in national collegiate championships (see Note 5):

Regatta	USA	Estimated Overseas	% USA	% Overseas
NCAA heavyweight women	706	< 60 ?	> 91%	< 9%
IRA heavyweight men, lightweight women	1.049	< 85	> 92%	< 8%
ACRA (no financial aid) men & women, mostly clubs, includes small boats	1,620	<20 ?	> 98%	< 2%
Total	3,375	<165	> 95%	< 5%

There are plenty of seats in college crews for our good young rowers. The problem is that after four years of rowing big sweeps boats, their potential for reaching the top level, in the small boats that dominate Olympic competition, is greatly reduced or gone forever.

The Collegiate Rowing Community

The money that flows to collegiate rowing supports a community of coaches and their athletic directors. Coaches and athletic directors, like any group whose livelihood derives from a common purpose, tend to resist outsiders. Change in college rowing can only come from within the collegiate rowing community, and fortunately, college competition can benefit by adding small boat events.

The Olympic goal of creating opportunities for smaller nations has a parallel in collegiate competition. If small boats were included in conference and national championship regattas (NCAA for women, IRA for men), the medal potential would be far better for smaller colleges. Coaches at small college programs would have a chance to shine at the national level. (see Note 6.)

Is this motivating? It should be, for the many coaches and athletic directors who are intensely competitive. But others place more weight on the non-competitive values found in rowing. Coaches can thrive by providing a positive life experience to their rowers: the satisfaction of learning a physical skill, the addictive appeal of the pull and glide, the beauty of still water at dawn, and the social pleasures of working as a team. A coach can be revered for processing an annual crop of graduates, with no victories but many fond memories.

As an example, a rowing coach at an NCAA Division III college recently retired after 26 years, during which he acquired numerous accolades, built his program from shared facilities to its own boat house, and assumed important duties as an official in the rowing establishment. No one would argue his contributions. In the course of his 26-year coaching career, at the annual regional regatta for colleges of similar size, his crews never finished better than 4th, and that was in 1997. Medals, for this coach, had nothing to do with his success.

In an environment where medals are nice but not important, it's unreasonable to expect enthusiasm for introducing small boats in order to broaden medal opportunities. On the contrary, any initiative to change a well-greased model is guaranteed to meet resistance.

On the other side are those coaches who strive to excel in competition, and athletic directors whose competitive success validates their judgment and their allocation of funds. They see winning athletes as an asset for college recruitment and alumni support. For their athletes, trying to excel teaches lessons that can't be learned from accepting mediocrity.

The merits of simple participation versus the merits of competition are a subject for honest debate, with valid arguments on both sides. The key to progress within the collegiate rowing community lies with competition-driven coaches and athletic directors, notably in the smaller institutions that can't expect to win in eights.

For USRowing, with its mandate as National Governing Body, the merits of competition must take precedence (see below, in the chapter on USRowing's obligations). But compared to the colleges, USRowing is a small tail on a very big dog.

Before considering what initiatives might help to wag the dog, it's useful to understand how other countries develop their talent, in the next chapter.

Notes to Chapter Two

Note 1 - In many countries, NGBs receive taxpayer support, but not in the USA. Individuals overseas pay higher taxes (value-added tax on sales, high marginal rates on income, social charges up to 60% of total hourly pay). High taxes are accepted with the understanding that government is responsible for supporting culture and sport. Most Americans prefer lower taxes and more discretionary income to support their own choices. As shown in the spending table, the result for rowing comes out about even in most countries, with an advantage for Britain. A good proportion of Britain's extra spending is for recruiting and supporting school kids who are potentially world class athletes

Note 2 – Please see Appendix C for comment on sources and assumptions. In brief, NGB budget estimations are gleaned from their websites; most are supported by personal correspondence. For other nations, the fraction devoted to competition is derived by comparing competition staff to total personnel, with a multiple applied for travel and facilities. No precision is claimed, but in your author's opinion, variances greater than 10% are unlikely.

USRowing's budgets are published. The fraction of 1/2 for competition is supported by USRowing's head count (See Note 2 to Chapter Four). It includes expenses assigned to our "National Team" and "Junior National Team", leaving out items in USRowing's "Domestic" budget for clinics, camps, coaching materials, etc. Our "U23" and Junior teams are largely rower-paid, and self-funding does not figure in the NGB total.

Note 3 – Germany was selected for comparison because top-to-bottom figures can be easily estimated. A similar comparison would apply for most other countries. German spending at the national team level seems light compared to similar expenditures by USRowing, but German clubs provide substantial support for national team rowers – their development system is club-based.

Note 4 – The IRA provides a venue for women's lightweight rowing, including double sculls. This sculling event represents a solitary exception to our all-sweeps regime in collegiate national championships.

Note 5 – The estimation of total overseas presence in US collegiate regattas is kindly provided by Gary Caldwell, Commissioner of the IRA regatta, using his best guesstimates based on his own records and results on Row2k and Regatta Central.

Note 6 - This concept has been promoted by Jim Dietz, women's coach at UMass-Amherst and Vice President of USRowing. Jim is an all-time great sculler who can demonstrate the benefit of learning in small boats. His women have been frequent medal winners in eights as well as small boats. He is a strong advocate of aligning college regattas with international boat classes.

- photo: Jim Dietz

UMass rowers in a quad, a double, a single, and coxed fours, showing that small boats can thrive in college rowing

Chapter Three
Champions Start Young – Retention and the Will to Win

Athletes in endurance sports reach their peak in their late 20's or even later, and rowing is no exception. But an examination of the age and the medal history of the men's "A" finalists at Rio yields some surprising facts.

Most high-potential rowers start winning World Championships and Olympics medals at an age when our young rowers are fresh out of college.

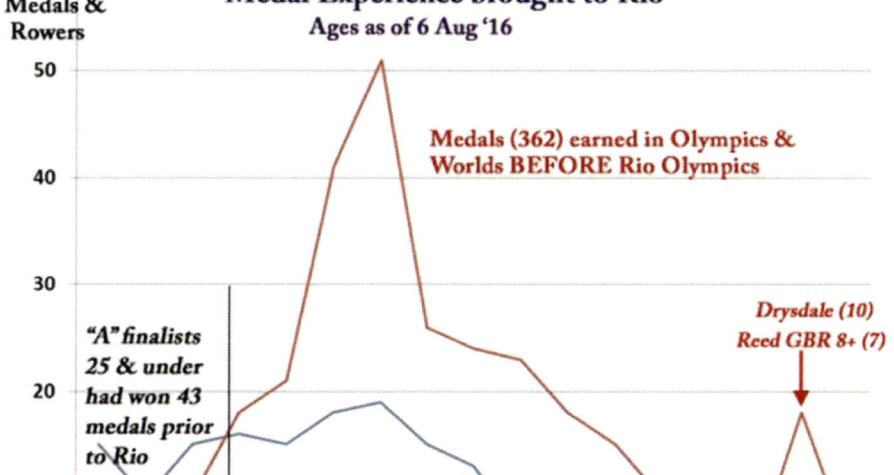

4 USA athletes had earned 7 medals before Rio, 2 in USA 8+, 2 in USA 4- ("B" final) their ages were 27 to 30

The longevity of perennial winners – Tufte, Drysdale, Murray & Bond, et al. – hides the youthful start of most champions, and there are exceptions (see Note 1).

The best rowers collect medals consistently as they grow from their early to their late 20's, as shown in the next table.

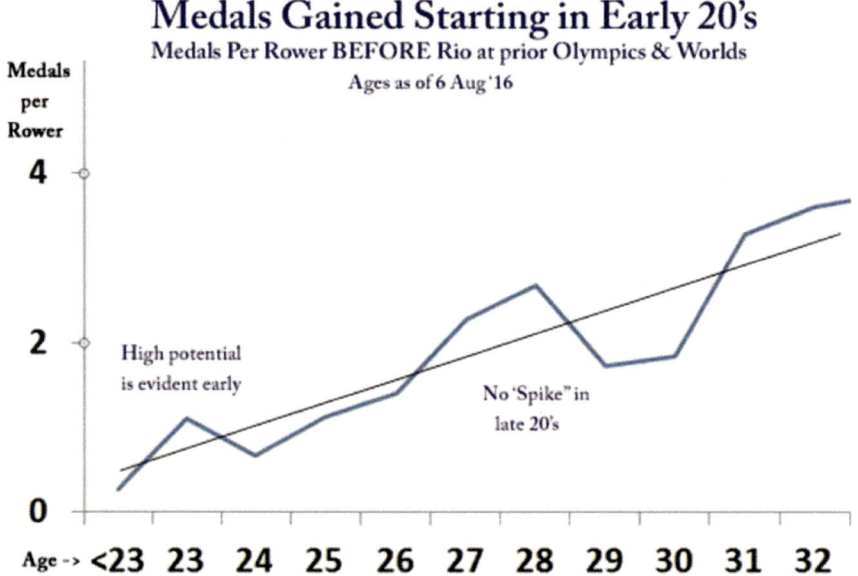

The "A" finalists show a steady progression of medals collected from their early 20's, before they qualified to row in Rio.

When all results are combined, a weak age/success relation is visible.

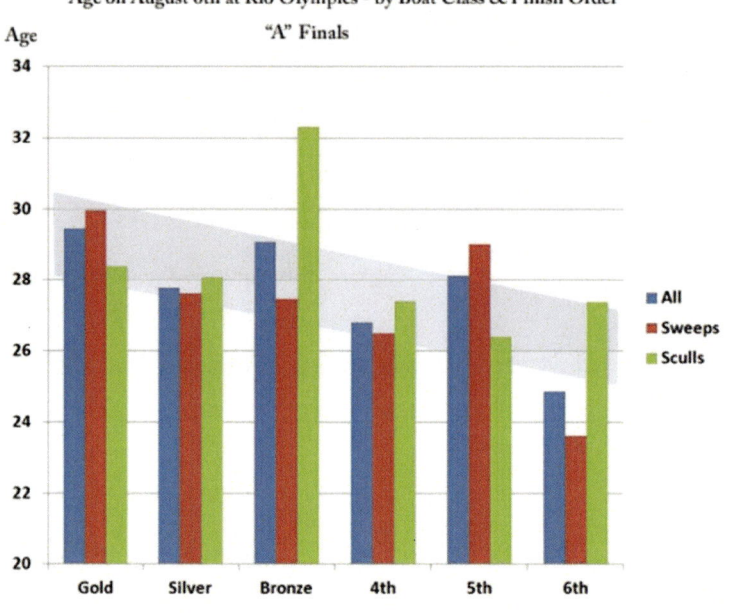

But the results for each event show that age is a poor predictor of success. Two boats aged just 23 won medals.

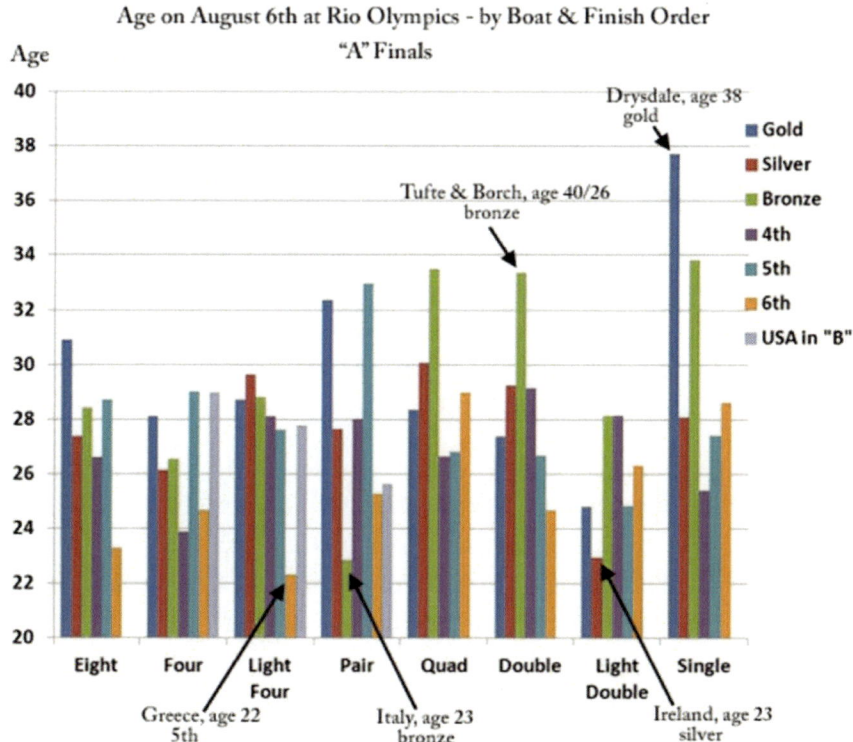

British depth should allow selection of the most mature athletes, and their winning eight was the oldest in the "A" final; their winning four was next oldest (after the Polish boat that finished 5th). But these oarsmen started young. The average age for the first Olympic or World Championship medal, earned by each of the 12 in the British eight and four, was just 24. Langridge, a 3x Olympic and 5x World Champion, all in sweeps, was World Champion Junior in singles.

It would be fine if we could take our top men from college and give them a crash course in small boats, using clubs and development camps as a base. If they are 23 or 24 now, they will be at their physical peak 4 years from now, at 27 or 28. The preceding suggests that this is way too late, and is likely to be disappointing. Especially because they are starting behind their contemporaries overseas, so their will to win will be frustrated in early days.

<u>Retention and the Will to Win</u>

Nowhere is retention more important than in collegiate club rowing. Unlike well-funded college programs, collegiate clubs without institutional sponsorship are paid for by the athletes. Athletes are almost all walk-ons who start with no experience and no incentives. Because the clubs exist on their dues, retention is existential.

The American Collegiate Rowing Association (ACRA) was founded to provide a venue for a national championship, when the Intercollegiate Rowing Association (IRA) excluded clubs (2008). Today the ACRA national championship has more participants than either the IRA, for men and lightweight women, or the NCAA for women.

Readers who are interested in retention will do well to refer to a how-to manual, "Building a Successful Collegiate Club Rowing Program" by Gregg Hartsuff. Gregg is the long-time, highly successful coach of the men's rowing team at the University of Michigan. The manual is available on line at:

(http://www.americancollegiaterowing.com/coaching_manual.html)

Two threads run throughout the manual. The first thread is shared by all enterprises – clear goals, no surprises, common-sense management, the cumulative effect of many small correct decisions. These all bear on individuals' attitude and motivation.

The second thread is competition's appeal to individuals who have the will to win. Some of Gregg's prescriptions are counter-intuitive in an organization that needs members, but they attract people who want to compete - such as an early 'try-out' where prospects need to survive an erg test.

Gregg emphasizes big boat sweeps for reasons specific to a dues-dependent, competition-driven organization – eights allow more rowers the satisfaction of rowing in the top boat, and competition in eights is perceived as the top challenge, above fours or quads, and way above singles or doubles. Gregg recognizes the importance of rowers who want to row without hope of a top seat, "if you have a sufficient number of rowers to occupy the bottom of the depth chart, it will help to anchor the competitiveness of the guys above them... if the guys above them are in eights, you can keep more guys."

Among Gregg's insights is the importance of big goals to keep athletes motivated. A "national" championship is big; other victories, not so much.

Gregg provides advice on the slower development of big rowers, quoted here:

"In my experience shorter, yet athletic and coordinated, athletes with smaller physiques pick up rowing technique much quicker than the tall, clunky guys. There is simply less mass to coordinate and they quickly bolt out in front in terms of overall speed value. Make everyone, especially the bigger novice guys, aware of this likely phenomenon. It may be well into the spring before the big guys are actually faster on the water due to differing development curves. This will keep the big guys encouraged; while at the same time won't discredit the good work the smaller athletes have done to get where they are."

This accurate observation leads to important questions – isn't it better to teach rowing <u>before</u> a big guy's full size fills in, i.e. starting in his mid-teens? This is not an option for college, but it is for our schools and for clubs, if they recruit big guys.

Gregg comments that sculling is easier than sweeps, because coordination is not needed between the two sides. Isn't it better to teach big guys in small sculling boats, where the learning curve is so much faster? Again, this is an option for schools and clubs.

Starting big kids when they are not yet big is surely one of the reasons why small-boat experience gives big boys from overseas an advantage over our big boys, whose development has been retarded in sweeps.

The conclusion is that athlete retention depends mostly on a promise of future success, in top competition (see Note 2). That promise can be supported by early personal achievement, or by competing on equal terms with teammates who have shown the way to win.

The preceding should not obscure the fact that money is important. As a practical matter, our elite rowers need enough money to train full time and be able to make ends meet. That should be an immediate goal. But, like other short-term fixes, it is not enough.

Offering the promise of success leads to a central theme of this book – to build a pool of high-potential young athletes with a clear path to the podium, by employing development practices that work elsewhere, and by encouraging collegiate competition to become an asset instead of a liability.

Notes to Chapter Three

Note 1 – Gevvie Stone didn't make the National Team for Beijing when she was 23. Four years later she was 7th (1st in the "B" final) in London. She took the Silver Medal in Rio, at age 31.

Helen Glover and Heather Stanning were 22 and 21 when they started rowing. They won gold medals in the pair for Britain, in London at ages 26 and 27, and in Rio at ages 30 and 31. (Both were products of Britain's START program.)

Similar examples of late-starting men are not evident.

Note 2 – Aiming for top honors is important for motivation, and collegiate top honors are in eights. But the example of the Head of the Charles shows that top honors are defined by who is in the event. At the Head of the Charles, Olympic medalists compete in Champ Singles, and singles winners get as much or more recognition than winners in eights.

Most adults in the rowing community assume that the supremacy of eights in college is cast in bronze. One says that trying to change it is like 'pushing on a string'. But if the best collegiate rowers were in singles, doubles, and pairs, the prestige of these events would be equal or superior to the eights, and highly motivating to keen competitors. In a perfect world, collegiate competition could be an incubator for international success.

Offering medals for individual events is one way to honor small boat victors. If coaches and athletic directors agree that leveling the playing field is good for collegiate rowing, this one step will provide medal opportunities for smaller programs that can never win in eights.

As well, team trophy points can be weighted to emphasize small boats. It should not be hard to devise a point system that encourages seating the strongest rowers in the smaller boats.

Chapter Four

Best Practices

In business, evaluating competitors' "best practices" is a necessity, but in the USA, more could be known about other nations' practices for rowing talent development, and some of what we think may not be true. Your author's research project, completed in the winter of 2016, led to a short list of best practices overseas. In summary:

<u>Best Practices</u>

1. Clear development path from initiation to elite, aimed at international success - no competing goals
2. Initiation in sculling boats
3. Best young rowers placed in small boats (1x, 2x, 2-), less best in bigger boats (4x, 4-, 8+)
4. Competition-driven national association (NGB)
5. Mandatory coach certification, national standards

Each of these provides specific benefits which we lack, as noted in the following pages.

Clear path – no competing goals

Coaches elsewhere see themselves as part of a national development process aimed at international success. To quote from the Germans,

> "*Nur gemeinsam sind wir schlagkraftig*"
>
> ("Only together are we powerful")

This contrasts with the USA. In the USA, scholastic and collegiate regattas define coaches' and athletes' success. Regional school competition may conflict with national junior regattas. College rowers need to complete their sweeps season before turning to national selections.

In the USA, recognition for international success comes only at the top of the pyramid, for our national team coaches and athletes.

In other countries, progress for a promising young rower is marked by international competition at the junior and U23 levels. The same is true for only a minority of young USA rowers, who, if selected, must find local funds to support their international participation.

The conflict of priorities would go away, if our schools and colleges competed in the international boat classes, because our coaches and our budgets would support training in these boats. Instead of taking a fork off the path, we would be on track with the rest of the world.

Initiation in Sculling Boats

This is true in all other countries, for clear reasons:

a. Sculling is easier on developing young bodies (this was one of the reasons cited for Britain's change)

b. In small sculling boats, the boat is the teacher, and efficient technique is more apparent. "Feel for the water" and waterman skills are part of learning

c. Transition from sculls to sweeps is so easy, it hardly deserves notice. Transition in the opposite direction takes more time, with unpredictable results

d. Sculling in singles or doubles gives visibility and challenge to individualists. We laud the team aspect of rowing, but some potentially great rowers may not be happy as a mule in harness

Rowing in a beginner eight is not fun. The majority of a beginner's time is spent hauling on the oar while idle rowers provide balance, wasting time on the water that should be spent rowing. With all eight rowing, crashing and bashing give no chance of individual feedback. Even when gross anomalies start to work out, individuals still can't sense and respond to feedback from their own activity. When a crew's technique improves enough to move an eight at speed, it goes too fast to perfect the millisecond timing of blade entry and drive.

Because most of our young rowers row in big boats where technique is hard to appreciate, erg scores are often taken as a proxy for potential speed on the water. Maybe because of this focus on erg results, American crews are sometimes criticized for poor technique compared to overseas rivals.

It is a given that a championship crew needs both technique and power. Which is more important?

From James Tomkins, an Australian 3x Olympic gold medalist and 7x World Champion – *""At the end of the day, everyone is pretty much as fit and strong as one another. It comes down to how you actually row,"* i.e. efficient technique makes the difference. But we have the example of our women's eight in London, who powered their way to a gold medal. The picture below was taken at 500 meters in their race to gold. If 4 and Stroke are good, what can we say about 2 and 6? (Our women's eight in Rio looked more united.)

freeze frame: YouTube London Olympics Women 8+ final

It may be possible to win by overpowering weaker crews, but in the long run, James Tomkins is correct. In most races, power balances out between the crews, and the most efficient technique wins.

Many college coaches now train their rowers in pairs, for all the reasons noted above. This makes sense, but it comes late. Done to excess, it may be counterproductive, because neural triggers honed in a pair may not adapt well to the speed of an eight.

Best Young Rowers Placed in Smaller Boats

This is explicitly stated in Germany, but emphasis on small boats in other countries suggests that it applies equally in many places.

It's a better bet to develop small boat champions::

- ... The likelihood of unforeseen issues (illness, injury, etc.) increases exponentially with the number of rowers in the boat

- ... Races between small boats are more predictable. In the diagram, the speed differential is identical in percent but the eight race could still turn into a nail biter. The single is too far behind to catch up.

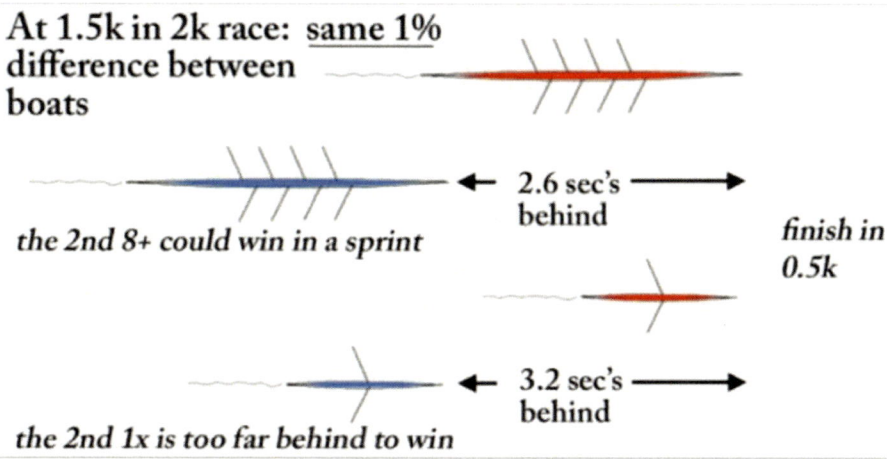

- ... Top small boat rowers seem to be more durable, with many repeat medalists at successive Olympics

Putting the best rowers in the smaller boats is 180° opposite from historical USA practice, where the best rowers are seated in eights.

There is always an opportunity to find winning combinations, by putting excellent small boat rowers into big boats, and some US colleges use pairs metrics to guide selection for their eights. But transition from big boats to small, at the elite level, is unsure at best.

Competition-led national association

Elsewhere, NGBs and rowing organizations put international competition first. Outreach and community are often part of their stated goals, but they are subordinate to the goal of international success.

This makes sense. Sports become attractive when role-model athletes win for their country (see Note 1). <u>The best way to encourage outreach, inclusion, longevity and community is to succeed in international competition.</u>

In the USA, rowing remains a sport for individuals who can pay their own way. "Inclusion" as a goal is not coherent, when our rising talents must pay to compete. A talent path aimed at international competition needs support for promising athletes as well as for proven elites.

Britain's START program, lottery funded, recruits promising juniors and helps them on the development path. In the USA, a competition-driven program aimed at finding and developing international winners might earn corporate sponsorship to rival Britain's START funding.

USRowing's obligations include the need to put competition first in the list of priorities. <u>International success will enhance and not diminish other worthy goals.</u>

Chapter Six discusses governance and management at USRowing. To compare with other countries is difficult, but personnel rosters are available on some countries websites. Compared to other countries, USRowing has the lowest percentage of staff devoted to competition. (see Note 2).

Mandatory coach certification

CRI's Institute of Rowing Leadership offers a post-graduate education in coaching, and USRowing offers coach certification and coaching videos – but only a fraction of the 2,500 coaches in the USA have such certification.

Germany, Italy, and other countries require certification for club as well as national team coaches.

At regattas in the USA, most young sweeps crews are visibly not ready to race. Except for a top-seeded few, the 'wounded centipede' boats could be rowed better with better coaching. Kids in Europe are taught to row by qualified coaches, with direction from their NGB.

Where our juniors find good coaching, they are as good as any in the world. At the 2016 Junior Worlds in Rotterdam, two well-coached girls from the Quad Cities won gold in a sculling boat. But overall, our boys and girls don't learn to row as well as their foreign contemporaries because so many coaches have little training. The difference in technique is not because European or British kids are more gifted than ours. It's because they start in small boats with qualified coaches.

freeze frame: Jim Dietz

A drill in singles – why can't more rowers get this kind of training?

Note to Chapter Four

Note 1 – In the USA, Arnold Palmer's success in the British Open, Jimmy Connors' and John McEnroe's Grand Slam titles, Billy Kidd's and Spider Sabich's ski wins in the Alps, all led to explosive growth in their sports, with a transformation from 'country club' participation to the public at large.

Rob Waddell and the Evers-Swindell twins helped turn New Zealand into a hotbed of rowing talent. (NZ's population is equal to Metro Boston, NZ wins more medals than the USA)

Note 2 – The following graphs show personnel devoted specifically to competition and to general administration, member services, etc., for USRowing and for the NGBs in other countries which provide roster information. We devote the least share of our NGB staff to competition.

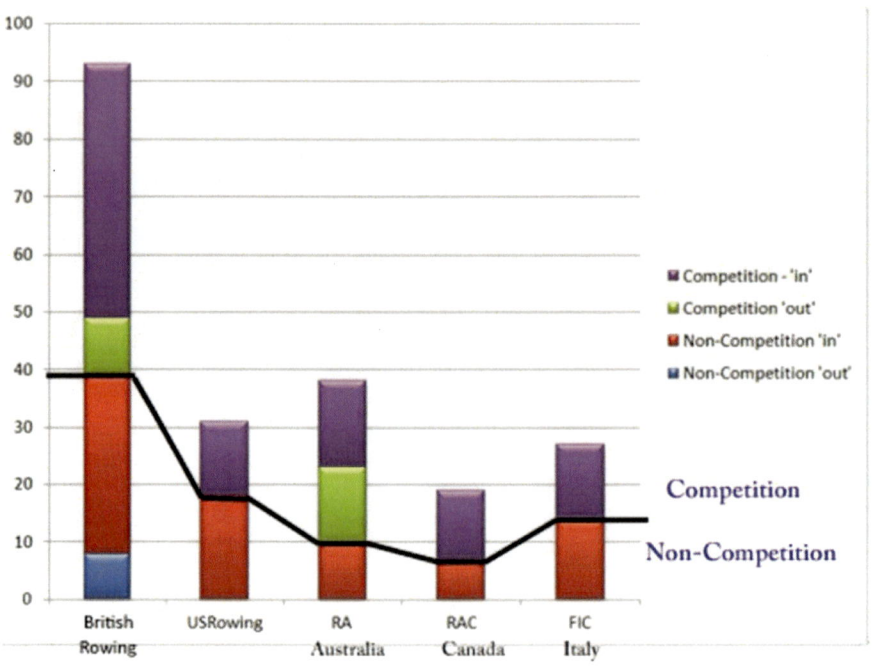

"In" includes headquarters & training centers
"Out" includes area & regional people e.g. Britain's START

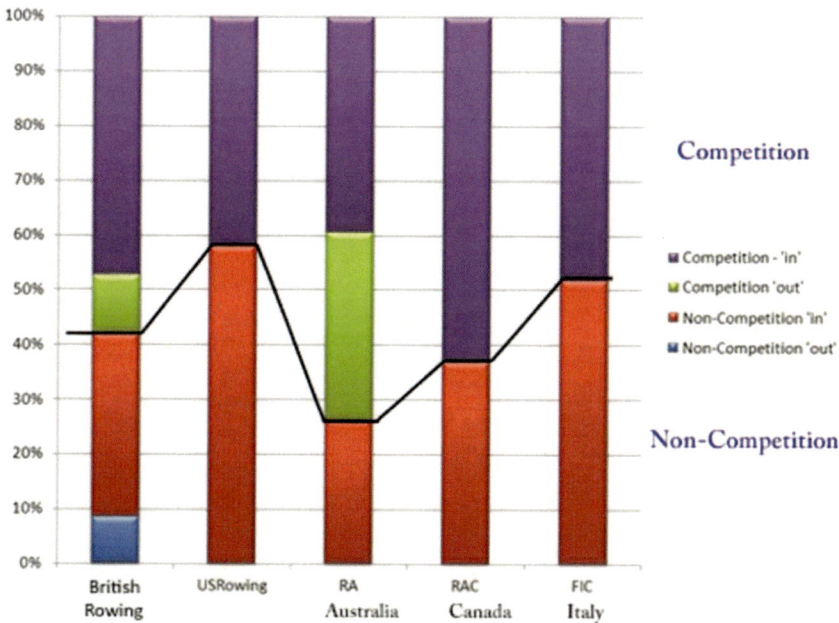

Chapter Five
Dots of Light on a Dark Continent

We are making progress, slowly but truly. A growing number of clubs and schools are focused on small boats, and our international bright spots in Junior and U-23 competition are due to them. The bright spots are still too few, and they are far outnumbered by sweeps-only programs.

The graphic below illustrates areas where juniors start in small boats – represented by dots of light. The map is generalized, with apologies to any area deserving a dot that doesn't have one.

As the cluster of dots in the Mid-Atlantic area suggests, junior rowing in small boats has progressed furthest there, with many school rowers competing in sculling boats.

School crews in New England row sweeps. New England schools lag behind the rest of the nation, and the outlook there is as bleak as the college picture. Clubs in Boston, Providence, and Connecticut take up some of the slack for school-age rowers.

To show the overall imbalance of junior sweepers in excess of junior scullers, it's convenient to look at participation in school-age races.

Junior sweepers outnumber scullers everywhere, even in the Mid-Atlantic area.

... At the largest high school regatta, the Stotesbury Cup, and at the Head of the Schuylkill, both held in Philadelphia, sculling representation is relatively good.

... The Head of the Rock, in Rockville, IL, is a well-attended Mid-West regatta with rowers from as far away as Missouri and Michigan. There, the proportion of junior scullers is less than in Philadelphia.

...At the Textile River Regatta in Massachusetts, junior sweepers far outweigh junior scullers, especially amongst the boys. Dark indeed...

Junior sweepers / junior scullers	Boys	Girls
Stotesbury Cup (PA)	4.0x	4.4x
Head of the Schuylkill (PA)	3.4x	3.6x
Head of the Rock (IL)	7.8x	6.5x
Textile River Regatta (MA)	17.3x	11.9x

It is a shame that NEIRA, New England's Interscholastic Rowing Association, with its 80+ member schools and its century of rowing history, competes only in fours and eights.

NEIRA schools, with some others, do not offer rowing as a fall sport. Their eight or nine weeks on the water are not sufficient, although schools lacking rowing as a fall sport frequently enter fall head races, notably the Head Of The Charles®, where scholastic events enjoy the biggest fields. This is better than leaving boats and facilities idle for half the school year.

Without disparaging football or soccer, many kids, like some great rowers who have lacked the coordination to excel in ball sports, might be happier rowing in the fall.

Training and competition for young rowers in the Olympic small boat classes is offered by:

- USRowing's Training Center Partners for U-23 and elite rowers, training in small boats. Most include juniors:

    California Rowing Club, Oakland, CA
    Community Rowing, Inc., Brighton, MA
    Craftsbury Sculling Center, Craftsbury Common, VT
    GMS Rowing Center, New Milford, CT
    Long Beach Rowing Association, Long Beach, CA
    The New York Athletic Club, Pelham, NY
    Penn A.C. Rowing Association, Philadelphia, PA
    Pocock Rowing Center, Seattle, WA
    Potomac Boat Club, Washington, DC.
    Riverside Boat Club, Cambridge, MA
    SoCal Scullers, Huntingdon Beach, CA
    Vesper Boat Club, Philadelphia, PA

- Other clubs and camps that initiate, coach and promote juniors and U-23's in competition
- Many private and some public schools, with variation depending on area
- The American Collegiate Rowing Association (ACRA) – member-paid college clubs, some with college support
- Some NCAA/IRA colleges with coaches who believe in the benefits of small boat competition

Although school rowers far outnumber club juniors nationally, 22 clubs and just 6 schools sent rowers to the 2016 Junior World Championships in Rotterdam. Our Junior Team's affiliations are listed here:

Berkeley High School (CA)*	Narragansett (RI)
California Yacht Club (CA)	Nashville-St Cecilia (TN)*
Capital City (FL)	NorCal (CA)
Cathedral Catholic High School (CA)*	Oakland Strokes (CA)
Connecticut Boat Club (CT)	OKC Riversport (OK)
Dallas United (TX)	Rose City (OR)
Deerfield (MA)*	RowAmerica Rye (NY)
GMS (CT)	San Diego (CA)
Gonzaga High School (PA)*	Sarasota (FL)
Long Beach (CA)	Saugatuck (CT)
Marin (CA)	Seattle (WA)
Marina Aquatic (CA)	Skyline Crew (MI)*
Maritime (CT)	Upper Natoma (CA)
Montclair High School (NJ)*	Y Quad Cities (IL)

* school, the rest are clubs

Our U23 team at Rotterdam included rowers from 10 clubs and 14 colleges (college rowers were at liberty after the collegiate sweep season). The rowers' affiliations are listed here:

College	Club
Brown University	Cambridge Boat Club (MA)
Columbia University	Conshohocken Rowing Club (PA)
Cornell University	Craftsbury Sculling Center (VT)

Ohio State University	Narragansett Boat Club (RI)
Princeton University	Olympia Area Rowing (WA)
University of California	Pittsford Crew (NY)
University of Michigan	Riverside Boat Club (MA)
University of Pennsylvania	Saratoga Rowing Assoc.(NY)
University of Texas	Undine Barge Club (PA)
University of Virginia	Princeton Nat'l/Mercer (NJ)
University of Wisconsin	
Yale University	
Newell Development Camp (Harvard)	

Imagine the collegiate competition for selection to our National U23 team, if small boats were an integral part of IRA and NCAA regattas, and imagine the results our U23 team might have against the rest of the world.

Other initiatives are chipping at the status quo. The Head of the Charles® in 2016 included youth quads for the first time, in addition to youth doubles and a collegiate division in the Championship Singles events. This support is important and commendable at the world's largest and most prestigious head race regatta.

2016 saw a November head race for men's pairs from colleges rowing on the Charles.

Jim Dietz at UMass Amherst and like-minded college coaches are proposing a fall calendar of collegiate women small boat racing. Colleges represented in last year's regatta were:

Cornell	Amherst	Rhode Island
Ithaca	Radcliffe	UMass–Amherst
Northeastern	Syracuse	

Real progress will come when financial aid is awarded to student-rowers who can excel in small boats, at the regattas that crown national champions in the NCAA and IRA.

Division III colleges and the ACRA clubs do not offer financial aid. They are not bound by tradition to sweeps, and ACRA certainly figures in any appreciation of collegiate rowing, with more participants in its national regatta than either NCAA or IRA. Unhappily, the absence of financial aid puts these programs out of competition for capable scholastic rowers who are attracted by a four-year free ride to a diploma. Also, the same factors locking schools into sweeps apply equally to Division III collegiate programs.

ACRA clubs, which depend on dues, have an added reason to focus on eights, to support and motivate larger numbers of dues-paying athletes. ACRA's small boat participation is light relative to sweeps. At the 2016 ACRA regatta, sweepers outnumbered scullers by a ratio of 14 to 1 for men, and 13 to 1 for women. Even more telling is the performance of ACRA pairs, which are 5% faster than ACRA doubles. Normally, doubles should be 2% -3% faster than pairs.

Could NGB encouragement and support help build Division III and ACRA programs into sources for international medalists? This seems like a long-shot, lacking financial aid to attract top-tier scholastic rowers.

But a shift to favor small boat competition, with a team point structure to encourage putting the best rowers into the smaller boats, would change the picture.

Can we wait for the best college rowers to graduate before we prepare them to compete in the international boat classes? As noted in Chapter Three, it is most likely too late.

Chapter Six
USRowing's Obligations

USRowing has functioned as a service organization, addressing the needs of its members. It has been good at providing training, information, and regattas. Our Masters regattas are the best run in the world. Making routine things happen in a routine way gains little applause, but management has deserved compliments for a smooth running operation.

As a service organization, USRowing has provided structure for our National Team, including selection of coaches and athletes, venues for training, and decisions concerning which crews to support. After Rio, all of these have been subject to review, and recent changes signal the will to change for the better. But changes which are limited to our elite programs will be unlikely to produce long term progress.

As a service organization, USRowing has responded to changing needs, e.g. support of Adaptive rowing, but the effort has been essentially reactive, not proactive. USRowing has not been an advocate for change. But to catch up with the rest of the world, no one else was responsible, and we have fallen behind.

USRowing's obligations as NGB are outlined here.

...   The U.S. Olympic Committee (USOC) has a mandate from Congress, the "Ted Stevens Act". This mandate grants monopoly status and shelter from certain lawsuits. USOC delegates its mandate to the NGB for each sport, and each NGB is obligated by the provisions of the Ted Stevens Act.

...   The Ted Stevens Act asks for "<u>the most competent amateur representation possible</u> in <u>each event</u> of the Olympic Games, the Paralympic Games, and Pan-American Games"

   "Most competent possible" means seeking ways to excel. Otherwise the Act would ask for NGBs to obtain the "best available" representation.

... Our men's dismal results in Rio speak for themselves. We have failed in the one clear statement of USRowing's role concerning international competition, "to continually improve performance at the Olympic Games" (please see Note 1 for USRowing's Mission Statement).

... And, despite "every event" as cited in the Ted Stevens Act, we were absent from all men's open sculling events (single, double, and quad). Our lightweight men's double was our only sculling entry.

... The Act includes goals intended to develop talent from initiation to elite. Simply selecting the best candidates from a pool of mid-level athletes is not sufficient.

To fulfill its obligations as NGB, USRowing needs to address the entire talent development process from initiation, with standards to measure progress at each level. USRowing needs to influence, as best it can, talent development outside its control.

The concluding chapter on achieving our potential suggests positive ways to encourage change *outside* USRowing. The first changes should be internal, concerning mission and governance, starting with the Board of Directors and including management, to convert USRowing from a passive service organization to a proactive advocate for positive action.

An Amended Mission

USRowing's Mission Statement should recognize its obligations as NGB. The following Mission Statement is suggested for content; other words to the same effect might be better:

Mission. The mission of USRowing is to fulfill its obligations as National Governing Body, and to promote rowing in the United States by all practical means.

In pursuit of this mission, USRowing will seek means to:

a.   Develop rower talent from initiation to elite

> b.   *Provide the most competent representation possible in each event of the Olympic Games, the Paralympic Games, and Pan-American Games*
>
> *c., d., e., etc. ... other objectives*

Governance

Most successful organizations find ways to deal with the healthy tension between positive change and a smooth-running operation. (See Note 2). If USRowing had achieved this balance years ago, our men might have done better in Rio.

USRowing's CEO has been focused on existing needs and not on shaping the future. That would have been O.K., if a roadmap to the future had come from the Board of Directors.

But without such a road map, USRowing was bound to the status quo, i.e. failure to provide the most competent representation possible in international competition.

It is not the role foreseen by the Ted Stevens Act, nor is it sufficient to meet USRowing's obligations as NGB.

The Board of Directors

To address this problem, USRowing's directors should amend the By-Laws' Mission Statement, recognizing USRowing's obligations as NGB (along the lines described above).

At the time of this writing, the future composition of the Board is a question mark. The By-Laws provide for several committees, including High Performance Committees for Juniors, U-23's, and Elites. While legal considerations may underlie this structure, it makes little sense otherwise. High performance goals are central to the role of an NGB, and governance should be taken over by the Board. This implies directors who are knowledgeable and involved in competition issues.

Note 3 outlines the 14 directors as designated by the By-Laws. The composition of the Board is less important than including individuals who are informed and involved, with a common goal to change the face of competitive rowing in the USA.

Management

Should USRowing have a CEO and a COO, i.e. an individual on top who sets the road map, and another individual to make everything work? This structure seems top-heavy for an operation so small.

Instead, it would be better for the Board to charge management with long-range competition-driven goals, and let the CEO delegate the 'make it work' functions to others. The CEO's time can then be spent bringing proposals to potential corporate sponsors, cementing relations with existing sponsors, building connections with collegiate and scholastic decision-makers, and communicating directly with leaders at clubs, training centers, and outreach/recruitment programs.

The CEO should prepare plans to achieve the Board's goals, for the Board's approval. Plans should include:

- ... specific tasks to be completed, with measurable standards
- ... budget and source of funds
- ... date(s) of completion, including key steps
- ... the individual assuming responsibility

A 'plan' lacking these elements is only wishful thinking ((this is from "Management 101").

The Board has a responsibility to follow up, with periodic reports coming from the CEO and responsible individuals.

Money

Presently, USRowing receives revenue from a variety of sources, noted below.

The National Rowing Foundation (NRF) raises money from a group of generous individuals. Its charter limits its role to charitable contributions, i.e. excluding sponsorships. USRowing also solicits individual donors, but the NRF is the main source of private contributions.

USRowing has corporate sponsors, but their role has been less important than other revenue sources. Here is the 2016 revenue breakdown, from USRowing's website:

USRowing Revenues

	2015	2016
Contributions	47,000	105,000
Grants & USOC Funding	3,267,497	3,631,895
Including NRF	*1,200,000*	*1,300,000*
Sponsorship	914,350	953,350
Events	845,000	871,500
Dues	2,235,450	2,533,255
Sales	425,000	511,400
Entry Fees & Regatta's	1,530,250	1,910,270
Other	145,115	212,451
Investment Activity	6,700	8,700
Total Revenues	9,416,362	10,737,821

"Sponsorship" has come from a group of loyal business supporters and payments from regatta venues. Large sponsorships from major companies are missing. (The Head of the Charles® raises more money from corporations than USRowing.)

Fund raising is an important part of any non-profit CEO's job. The CEO is the organization's face for potential sponsors. In addition, the organization must be staffed to make sponsorship attractive, both in presentation and in execution.

- ... sponsors typically spend substantial additional amounts to get the benefit of their investment, on top of their outlay for the sponsorship itself. Ratios of 1x to 3x additional spending are normal
- ... sponsorship is more attractive if the sponsor's investment includes public awareness activity to ensure high visibility, (what the Head of the Charles describes as 'activation') without further cost to the sponsor
- ... providing for high sponsor visibility is a win-win, because visibility is shared by sponsor and sponsored

USRowing is not staffed for this, but it could be. The last chapter, on achieving our potential, suggests programs that could attract sponsors by offering distinct naming opportunities.

As a cautionary note, although acquiring sponsors can be outsourced, no brand-marketing company can match the passion and insight that comes from within. And, typically, outside overheads take too much from any resulting revenues.

Vibrant success is attractive. Added to the other virtues of our sport, a competition-driven USRowing can find sponsors for new programs that would otherwise be unaffordable.

Notes to Chapter Six

Note 1 – USRowing's present By-Laws include a Mission Statement which gives scant attention to competition. From today's By-Laws: –

"<u>Mission</u>. The mission of USRowing is to provide ongoing opportunities to achieve excellence in rowing in the United States. In pursuit of this mission, USRowing will achieve the following results:

"... Steadily increase awareness of rowing

"... Consistently grow lifetime participation in rowing

"... Provide education on rowing safety, healthy training methods, and effective rowing technique

"... Provide standards for all rowers of safe, fair racing

"... Continually improve performance at the Olympic Games

"... Maintain fiscal growth and responsibility "

Inconsistencies in the By-Laws suggest that no one reads them, but a new mission statement to replace the preceding will focus on becoming a competition-led organization.

Note 2 – Most large corporations have a CEO who points the way to the future, and a COO who makes everything work. Even small organizations often have a *de facto* balance, e.g. between the CEO and the Chief Financial Officer or some other senior executive. All change is disturbing. It is hard for a single individual to initiate important changes while ensuring that routine things happen in a routine way.

Note 3 - The Board has consisted of 14 Directors,

- 2 - the President and Vice Chair, elected by individual USRowing members
- 4 - are athlete/AAC/USOC-related
- 2 - are at-large, elected by the other directors
- 6 - one from each of the six regions, elected by the 1,300 member organizations

The constitution of the Board is partly dictated by requirements for recognition as NGB.

Chapter Seven
Achieving Our Potential as a Rowing Nation

The burden must fall on USRowing, to justify its NGB status.

USRowing should do everything possible to optimize the present selection/coaching/training process for elites, i.e. short term solutions at the top of the ladder. This is fundamental.

The more pressing need is to start now on long-term goals. Here are three:

1. Recruit and develop young rowers with elite potential
2. Initiate rowers in sculling boats
3. Align boat classes at NCAA and IRA regattas with the boats rowed in the Olympics

Other goals such as coach certification and athlete retention may result from success with the three noted above.

Big Money

Few sports can embellish a corporate image better than ours. Rowing's positive associations include teamwork, fitness, and financial independence. These attributes are highly attractive for building corporate identity.

Rowing is surprisingly visible considering the few who actually row. As in the preceding clipping, a Wall Street Journal article on Harvard's endowment performance (nothing to do with rowing) is illustrated with a sculler approaching Weeks Bridge. Rowing's visibility is an asset that adds value for a sponsor.

Rowing is fortunate to have a substantial number of enthusiasts who are active in the financial community, where contacts and relationships play a vital role. Sponsorships can provide access within this community.

It should be USRowing's task to package programs that can carry corporate identification, i.e. "naming opportunities". Here are two suggestions for the imaginary "Willworth Company".

"Willworth Scholarships", awarded to the top three male and top three female graduating scholastic scullers, providing full tuition at the college of their choice while they continue to compete in sculling boats. ($ 350,000 compounding to $1,250,000 annually including $ 50,000 internal public awareness support)

"Willworth Grants" to defray costs of clubs recruiting juniors with elite potential, including expenses of the selected juniors. ($ 1,000,000, with a provision for internal public awareness support)

Good minds abound in the rowing community. Thoughtful, goal-oriented ideas are needed to win corporate support.

Small Money

USRowing cannot instruct the NCAA Rowing Committee, or the IRA stewards. Unwelcome push may invoke the 'law of unforeseen consequences' where push-back results in an unwanted outcome. With attention and care for sensitivities, USRowing can and should appeal to the interests of those concerned, by building contacts, understanding issues, and encouraging like-minded individuals.

USRowing can use the truth to win minds and encourage change. Creating a public awareness program is not free, but it can be done within USRowing's present budget framework.

The boat-class issue should be publicized within the rowing community by features and photos <u>with USRowing endorsement</u> placed on Row2k, Rowing News and social media.

<u>Foreign dominance in our college crews should be publicized, along with the reasons</u> – not with the idea of keeping foreign students out, but with the goal of bringing US students up to a competitive level.

Where independent initiatives are going the right way, USRowing should provide support. Examples:

... if a group of colleges puts together a fall small boat championship (the Jim Dietz initiative), USRowing can help with venue identification, officials, and logistic support, and can ensure that winners are amply recognized

... where an inner-city outreach program is working, USRowing can actively encourage emulation at other city clubs.

USRowing can work with schools to encourage small boats, and can work with equipment providers to create economies. As an example, for sub-Juniors (14 & under), the Italian federation endorses a monotype single. Materials are specified, to control cost. Like many one-design sailboats, the shells are provided by multiple boat builders, to ensure pricing competition. Oars have "Macon" tulip blades. Compared to hatchets, they tick wavetops less on the recovery and don't lock in on the drive – better for learning.

Standard hulls, Macon blades

At the Kinderskiff regatta held the day before Silverskiff, around 300 kids aged 14 and under compete in a 4 km head race. Considering their age, their technical level shows strong coaching.

It's a safe bet that Kinderskiff participants of 8 to 12 years ago were competing for Italy in Rio, where their men put four boats in "A" finals, compared to our two. It's interesting that Italy's two medals were both earned in sweeps, the light four and the pair. Their kids learned in singles and they beat ours in sweeps. Hmm...

If the Italian federation can push at the initiation stage, why can't USRowing? A simple modest target would be to encourage conversion of scholastic coxed fours to coxed quads.

Would it be a step too far, for USRowing to say that, as of 2020, USRowing-sanctioned regattas would no longer admit rowers in sweep boats who had not passed their 16th birthday as of January 1st? Today, this would be widely rejected. With understanding that college financial aid goes first to strong rowers who are technically skilled, that might change.

USRowing could urge organizers at sanctioned school regattas to put coxed quads and coxed fours in the same events – this sounds outrageous, but a good scholastic four will beat all but the five or six best quads. The challenge would most likely result in student pressure to convert from coxed fours, a very positive outcome.

All of these notions assume that USRowing becomes an advocate, and not simply a service organization.

Appendix A - College spending for rowing

2015 Collegiate spending ($'000)

	Men	Women			Women only
grand total -> 95,253.2	23,265.8	71,987.3			
IRA & NCAA	19,029.9	24,071.8		NCAA (no men)	22,297.1
Boston University	1,092.6	1,344.1	Div I	Boston College	592.6
Brown	550.1	479.5		Duke	1,599.8
California	1,260.3	1,048.9		Indiana	1,102.7
Columbia	442.6	275.9		Kansas	1,279.9
Cornell	700.1	319.3		Kansas State	1,030.8
Dartmouth	740.6	300.2		Michigan	1,951.7
Drexel	811.5	608.2		Minnesota	1,126.9
Florida Tech	335.9	170.3		Notre Dame	1,473.5
George Washington	371.6	499.4		Ohio State	1,989.5
Georgetown	460.8	426.7		Southern California	1,648.8
Gonzaga	501.9	553.6		Texas	1,600.1
Harvard	1,092.5	698.6		Tulsa	1,368.6
Hobart	183.3	194.8		UCF	1,226.8
Jacksonville	240.7	263.7		UMass	632.9
Marietta	82.0	80.7		UVA	1,653.6
Mercyhurst	372.7	329.1		Villanova	246.0
MIT	634.6	614.9			
Navy (est.)	500.0	500.0	Div II	Barry	445.9
Northeastern	1,270.7	1,273.8		Central Oklahoma	273.0
Oklahoma City	406.6	412.3		Nova Southeastern	701.9
Pennsylvania	569.9	541.7		Philadelphia	352.2
Princeton	771.0	789.6			
Santa Clara	101.1	119.9			Men	Women
Stanford	635.4	1,315.7			1,015.1	1,084.3
Syracuse	1,286.3	1,952.7	Div III	Bates	170.3	98.9
Temple	386.6	495.7	w/men's	Trinity	229.1	209.8
Washington	1,050.9	1,906.0	crew	Wellesley (est.)		200.0
Wisconsin	1,076.5	2,505.5		Williams	187.9	180.5
Yale	812.8	638.2		Hamilton	85.7	115.6
Pac 10 (in total above)				Washington College	165.6	115.7
Oregon State	288.0	1,096.6		Tufts	99.3	50.7
Washington State		1,221.3		Puget Sound	77.3	113.2
UCLA		1,094.9				

Spending in Ivy colleges appears to be less than spending by otherwise comparable non-Ivy institutions, for a reason. Ivy colleges do not grant "athletic scholarships". Although Ivy rowers' financial aid is omitted from Title IX calculations, they are quite likely to benefit from their college's aid pool.

"club" are rower-paid, not included in Title IX calculation

	Men	Women		Men	Women
Other Institutions	3,220.9	24,534.1			
Alabama		1,380.2	Duquesne		375.7
Binghamton	club		Endicott	club	
Bowdoin	club		Fairfield	121.3	142.6
Brandeis	club		Florida Tech	335.9	170.3
Brock	club		Fordham		642.3
Bryant	club		Franklin & Marshall		159.0
Bryn Mawr	club		Franklin Pierce	21.3	21.3
Buffalo		960.8	George Mason		418.2
Canisius		164.3	Georgia Tech	club	
Carnegie Mellon	club		Grand Valley	club	
Central Oklahoma		273.0	Hamilton	85.7	115.6
Charleston (WVA)		147.1	Haverford	club	
Cincinnati	club		High Point	club	
Clark	38.2	48.6	Holy Cross	238.0	383.8
Clemson		1,891.8	Iona		76.1
Colby	105.0	98.0	Iowa		1,269.3
Colgate	148.7	144.7	Ithaca	132.8	126.0
Connecticut		655.3	La Salle	159.5	170.4
Connecticut College	129.7	138.3	Lafayette	club	
Creighton		174.2	Lehigh		224.6
Dayton		177.7	Louisville		1,339.6
Delaware		659.2	Loyola Baltimore	108.6	96.7
DePaul	club		Manhattan	club	
Drake		192.1	Marist	103.1	257.7
Marquette	club		St Joseph's	314.2	350.6
Merrimack		69.6	St Lawrence	96.9	110.2
Miami		1,218.8	St Thomas (Minn.)	club	
Middlebury	club		Stetson	71.7	314.0
MSOE	134.5		Stevens	club	
NYU	club		Stony Brook	club	
Ohio University	club		SUNY Geneseo	club	
Old Dominion		1,140.7	SUNY Maritime	club	
Penn State	club		Susquehanna	club	
Purdue	club		TCNJ	club	
Robert Morris		345.6	Tennessee		1,435.5
Rochester Institute	84.7	84.3	UC San Diego	277.0	236.9
Rollins	162.2	127.0	Umass Lowell		155.7
Rutgers		628.2	UNC		438.2
Sacramento State		570.1	Virginia Tech	club	
Sacred Heart		127.3	Wentworth Inst.	club	
San Diego	165.1	793.1	Wesleyan	club	
San Diego State		804.6	West Virginia		746.2
Scranton	club		Western Washington		401.8
Simmons	club		Wheaton	club	
Skidmore	54.6	54.6	William & Mary	club	
Smith	club		WPI	132.4	107.9
SMU		1,178.8	College of Charleston	club	
St John Fisher	club				

Appendix B - A Narrative, October '15 to August '16

The January 20th resignations at USRowing included three of the four individuals who play a role in the following story. Of my interlocutors in 2016, only Jim Dietz, Vice-Chair of USRowing, remains. The narrative is retained here, because it illustrates the hurdles to overcome in the collegiate rowing establishment.

How this book began, and stops along the way

Over dinner in October of 2015, two of us were commiserating over our men's performance at the World Cup regatta held in Aiguebelette, France. Our eight had failed to qualify for inclusion at the Rio Olympics, leaving qualification in suspense until a 'Regatta of Death' in the spring. In our discussion, we noted that we had only foggy notions about foreign talent development, and that some of what we assumed might not be true. Because we share business backgrounds, we agreed that a review of 'best practices' elsewhere, compared with our own, might be useful.

So began my study, using the internet and personal contacts, to develop and compare 'best practices'. By the beginning of January a picture emerged that did, in fact, put a fresh perspective on our men's disappointing results, 'fresh' from its focus on the impact of collegiate spending on talent development. Conclusions from this study form the contents of Chapters Two and Four.

A key to unraveling perplexing situations, from my own business career, is to follow the money. This is where my research started, and the resulting comparison of money for talent development is not readily available from other sources.

Glenn Merry, CEO of USRowing, was very helpful in explaining USRowing's financial reports as shown on its website. In the process he gained not only my gratitude, but also my appreciation for his command of a buttoned-up, well-controlled operation. With my 'best practices' study in hand, I asked Glenn to review the conclusions with me, and early in February of this year, I visited him at USRowing's offices in Princeton. Glenn saw no issues to contradict my research and he kindly clarified some points.

At our meeting, we discussed what might be done with the study. Glenn suggested that I should meet with three key officers of USRowing, and sent them an email recommending that we meet. The three are:

... Erin O'Connell – President, presently an Associate Athletic Director at the University of Washington. Erin is a former cox and coach. Part of her background in athletics administration is 'compliance' concerning NCAA rules – more on this later.

... Jim Dietz – Male Vice Chair, and women's coach at UMass-Amherst, where he runs a strong small boat program that supports conference-winning big boats. I had had previous contacts with Jim and knew that anything to promote development in small boats would have a sympathetic ear.

... Gary Caldwell – Treasurer, and, until his retirement this year, the Director of Rowing at Tufts. Gary is Commissioner of the IRA. As Commissioner, he answers to seven Stewards who are Athletic Directors of IRA member institutions.

Glenn's introduction led to a telephone meeting with Erin O'Connell, after she had received a download copy of 'best practices'. She was receptive and positive in her response concerning the benefits of aligning NCAA championship events with Olympic boat classes. My bad hearing limits effective communication by phone, but Erin graciously followed up with a long, clear, and encouraging email, followed up by another email to answer some of my questions about NCAA's rules and definitions.

This was my first contact with the tangle of NCAA rules governing competition. In brief:

... NCAA rowing regattas fall under the NCAA 'team' definition (i.e. the champion is determined by combining results of 2 eights and a four; there is no special recognition for the best varsity eight). As

Erin explained, the 'team' designation allows "automatic qualification".

... "Automatic qualification" guarantees one entry for each of the eleven participating NCAA conferences. Without automatic qualification, the weaker conferences would not qualify for a national championship. With automatic qualification, eleven entries are filled by the best crew in each conference, and the remaining eleven entries are filled by the remaining best crews. Automatic qualification is universally accepted as beneficial.

... To make any change in the "team" format might defeat automatic qualification under NCAA rules.

Erin stressed that a change in format would require the agreement of the NCAA's Rowing Committee, that past initiatives to include small boats had not gained traction, and that any new initiative would need to be steered with great sensitivity and caution, to avoid negative reactions.

Erin suggested a survey of the collegiate rowing community, to be led by NCAA's Rowing Committee. The study would determine the degree of acceptance/resistance to changing the present regatta format.

A prerequisite for a survey would be resolution of how an individual sport format, akin to track & field, might impact automatic qualification. Erin suggested that one of the members of NCAA's Rowing Committee, an Athletic Director at UMass-Amherst, would be ideal to study the problem and, hopefully, clarify the question of automatic qualification.

The preceding made me understand that any change in the NCAA scheme would be difficult, but it seemed possible, given patience and care. The exchange with Erin preceded a meeting with Jim Dietz and Gary Caldwell, at the end of February. Before meeting Jim and Gary, I had hoped that substituting small boats at the IRA national championship regatta for men (e.g. quads and doubles for 4th and 5th varsity eights) should be less fraught with issues, because the IRA can write its own rules.

This meeting was a disappointment. To summarize:

… Neither Jim nor Gary argued the findings of my 'best practices' research, but the facts therein were perceived as irrelevant

… Gary explained that no collegiate small-boat initiative would succeed if it did not benefit the coaches and athletic directors involved, and, from that point of view, developing US talent for international success is a non-issue

… Gary discouraged any hope for change in IRA championship events

I complained that this seemed to leave out the kids and the public, but accepted Gary's objective appraisal and honesty.

At this meeting we talked about pending changes in Olympic boat classes, to be determined by the International Olympic Committee in May (two months after our meeting). We also talked about Erin's proposed NCAA survey, and the prerequisite study on automatic qualification. Jim, who is in contact with the Athletic Director at UMass-Amherst charged with the study, thought that the study should be completed by mid-May. It seemed best to wait until then to restart the discussion.

In the meantime, the objectives of Olympic competition were confirmed by FISA, the international governing body for rowing. These included the goals of inclusion and improving medal opportunities for smaller nations that are described in Chapter One.

A little background is needed here. Jim Dietz has been a longtime proponent of collegiate small boat competition. Long before the events described above, Jim had eloquently expressed a rationale for small boat events, based on improving medal opportunities for smaller colleges. This would allow more coaches and athletic directors to grow in esteem and support, and would help to justify rowing as a sponsored sport in smaller colleges. Personal interests could be advanced within the collegiate rowing community, as described in Chapter Two.

It seemed to me that the Olympic goals and Jim Dietz's goals were exactly parallel. I hoped that – for many coaches and athletic directors – matching Olympic and collegiate goals, to level opportunities for big and small, might provide impetus for aligning collegiate events with the international boat classes. In April I wrote to Erin to this effect. She replied that she would get back on the subject, but the query ended there. She also expressed her intention to see how the automatic qualification study was proceeding.

At the beginning of May 2016, I visited Jim at his beautiful new boat house in Amherst. We talked about managing a fleet of small boats, which seems to be a block for coaches who have never done it. We also talked about an advocacy group to formalize and expand his group of like-minded coaches.

May came and went. It seemed best not to pester my interlocutors while they were occupied with regatta season. Early in June 2016 I asked Jim if I should ask Erin to nudge the automatic qualification study. I subsequently did, and learned from her that she had thought Jim Dietz was pursuing the project. She commented that the first step continued to be determining whether women's rowing could be reclassified under NCAA's rules.

Jim went to Henley with his girl rowers and subsequently had a knee operation. During this period we were essentially out of contact. It turned out that both Jim and I incorrectly believed that Erin had launched the study on automatic qualification, maybe because it was her idea. The study had dropped between the cracks and never started.

At the end of August, Jim sent a long and thoughtful email, which I greatly appreciated. Essentially his conclusion was that changing the NCAA regattas was too hard, and that a better way was to develop a series of collegiate women's small boat regattas in the fall. Jim said that it was better to go slow.

As an outsider, I could only accept his wisdom. It's never a mistake to pick low hanging fruit before climbing a shaky ladder. I wrote back to offer my encouragement, but also expressed my disappointment that any question of changing the NCAA event format seemed dead. I expressed my belief that, without bringing small boats into the headline championship regattas, and without colleges awarding financial aid to potential sculling champions, the many junior programs where big boats prevail would be unlikely to change.

This ended our dialog. In the seven months from my first meeting with Glenn Merry, foreigners dominated in our top collegiate varsities, our men had a disastrous Olympics, and I could see no movement toward an effective solution.

At that point, I assembled the material that had accumulated, and started to write 'Boys in a Box'.

When Erin and I first talked, she asked me why I was doing this. It's a good question that I have asked myself. I didn't write down what I told her, but I remember offering these reasons:

First, recognizing symptoms in our men's rowing collapse that are common to underperforming organizations, as recalled from my business years. These are, acceptance of the status quo, resistance to internal change, and excuses aimed at external factors, especially about being outspent. These symptoms cry out for remedies.

Second, from rowing and racing in Europe, I can't avoid the notion that their adults are giving their kids a better deal.

And finally, having been left behind by boats I wanted to beat, I feel badly for our men. Facing the stern is worse than looking forward, because you lack any reference to the boats ahead. It's depressingly lonesome to get dropped, and surely worse after years of effort and sacrifice. It would be truly hard of heart not to empathize.

That's what I remember explaining, and maybe it displays too much sentiment for a tough world. Today I would add the upside, that I know no experience to match rowing the last five hundred meters of a race, when your mind escapes your body to say 'we can do it," and, in the last strokes, knowing that 'we did it'. It is a great feeling. The opportunity to share such moments can solve a lot of problems of recruitment and retention.

Why not make it possible?

Appendix C - Facts, sources, & assumptions

The thread of reason in "Boys in a Box" is based on comparing numbers – rowers, medals, dollars, etc.

For most comparisons, differences are so large that precision is hardly necessary, e.g. the amount spent on US collegiate rowing compared to the amount spent by USRowing or any other NGB.

Even if precision isn't essential, numbers need a basis in fact. Much of the time spent in preparing "Boys in a Box" was devoted to gathering facts and supporting reasonable estimates. The following describes how facts were sourced and assumptions made, so that readers can judge whether the resulting conclusions are justified.

Sources of facts are:

Medals – Wikipedia's record of results for each Olympics is excellent. Wikipedia is the source for individual medal histories as summarized in Chapter Three. (Yes, Wikipedia receives routine contributions from the author in recognition of its inestimable value.)

Overseas Crew Members in Top Varsities – Individual rower descriptions on many college rowing websites can be matched to the rowers named in that college's varsity. Cal and Yale, the top two IRA finishers, identify their varsity rowers, and their websites are the basis for the figure of 14 from overseas out of 16 total. Some college websites don't identify the rowers in their varsity, so this method can't be used to confirm Curtis Jordan's quote, that 30 out of the 48 rowers in the IRA Grand Final were from overseas. There is no uniform reporting requirement to identify nationality of collegiate rowers.

Collegiate Spending –Title IX compliance reports are a matter of public record. For convenience, the figures in Appendix A were drawn from an excellent website, www.collegefactual.com, which, for a small fee, provides extensive information for students researching college choices. CollegeFactual was used to look up spending on rowing by colleges found in Row2k's regatta results for 2015. If they didn't report race results they were omitted.

<u>USRowing's expenditures</u> – As a non-profit, USRowing's finances are a matter of public record. They can be found via the Governance links on the USRowing website.

Estimates were made as follows:

<u>The number of rowers in the USA</u> (Note 3 to Chapter One) – An on-line review generates figures for almost every sport, based on association membership, event participation, ticket sales, or equipment purchases.

Fortunately, this number is not critical for the reasoning in "Boys in a Box". No valid source exists for rowing, and opinions vary widely. Many propose 200,000 as the number of active US rowers, while Bruce Smith at CRI, when shown my 100,000 figure, said "If that...".

As a matter of definition, "rowers" should include individuals who use oars for propulsion while on a sliding seat, plus coxswains, and my sense is that at least 8 or 10 rows/year should be a minimum (the cutoff for inclusion among our 4.4 million erg rowers is 50x/year). Pararowers can object to the sliding seat criterion, and they should be included if a study is ever done.

Here is how 100,000 is projected:

<u>USRowing individual memberships (required for sanctioned regattas)</u>
age 26 and under	12,400
age 27 and over	6,400

<u>Collegiate rowers (35 rowers/coxes per program) rounded to nearest 1,000</u>
IRA (60 institutions)	2,000
NCAA (115 institutions)	4,000
ACRA (166 institutions)	5.000
Racers total	28,800

<u>Non-racing club rowers, in 271 clubs*,</u>	54.000

<u>200 rowers for each</u>

<u>Other rowers (off shore, solitary, etc.) – this is a plug to reach 100,000</u>	18,000
Rowers & coxswains total	~ 100,000

* Row2k lists 271 rowing clubs and this seems like the best source.

USRowing has 1,300 member organizations – a projection of 200,000 rowers/coxswains would be justified, if each member organization had 154. But half of the 1,300 organizations are schools or colleges, counted above. The other half include associations, booster clubs, and other entities which don't have rowers, or duplicate other rowing organizations.

It is apparent from the preceding that 100,000 is a stretch. A less optimistic figure would be in the range of 70,000 to 80,000 on water rowers.

<u>US Scholastic Budgets</u> – an average annual expenditure of $ 37,500 was used to project a total of $ 15 million for 400 schools. The average expenditure was reached after canvassing several schools and accepting large areas of uncertainty – should donated boats, tanks, buildings, etc. be included, and if so, should their cost be annualized for their service life? Should teacher/coach salaries be included, or apportioned? Should waterfront usage be assigned a value? How should student-paid extras be treated, e.g. spring break travel to Texas or Florida?

Recognizing that some schools with important rowing programs spend much more, the dollar figure used seems like a fair estimate. The number of schools is drawn from Row2K.

<u>US Club and Camp Budgets</u> – Many of the USRowing Training Partners, as well as clubs which sent Juniors to the National Selection regatta, responded to requests for their annual budgets. USRowing shows revenue for its camps, presumably equal to their cost, and a local

camp budget was defined. Overall, enough responses were gathered to generate projections with a reasonable level of confidence.

NGB budgets – Germany, Italy, Australia, New Zealand, and United Kingdom – budgets for these NGBs are not available on line, and a deductive process was required, with the exception of New Zealand.

New Zealand's budget for the 2012-2016 Olympic cycle was published by the NZ Herald in December 2012, at NZ $ 18.4 million. This translates to an annualized NZ $ 4.6 million. A subsequent YouTube, since disappeared, claimed a boost to NZ $ 5 million, equal to US $ 3.5 million. The on-line address of the NZ Herald article is:

http://www.nzherald.co.nz/sport/news/article.cfm?c_id=4&objectid=10854859.

Germany's Federation budget was obtained from a friend of a friend within the Federation. It appears to be accurate, given the importance of German clubs in the development process. The 263 German clubs were assigned as A (71) or B (192) depending on their size and importance; a multiple was applied, of US $ 150,000 for A's and US $ 25,000 for B's, to arrive at the total of US $ 15,450,000 for talent development.

For the UK, Italy and Australia (as for the USA) detailed rosters appear on their websites. Throughout the developed world, people at similar levels cost similar amounts, although the division of salaries versus benefits may vary. NGB rosters were used to develop total people costs. A multiple was added for overheads and travel, and this total was then offered for confirmation to individuals within the respective NGBs. (This seemed like a more tactful approach than simply asking for their budget, and the method produced positive responses.) The rosters also provided insight as to the division of tasks within each NGB.

In addition, reference was made to on-line news reports and announcements. For the UK, lottery funding is published on line at "https://www.uksport.gov.uk/our-work/investing-in-sport/current-funding-figures". For the four years from 2017 until 2020 British Rowing will receive £ 32.6 million, plus £ 3.2 million for ParaRowing. This equates to an annualized total of US $ 11.2 million at today's post-Brexit rate of exchange, or US $ 12.5 million before devaluation. Expenditure in the preceding four years was 10% less (no longer published on line). The difference between these figures and the estimated BRA total of US $ 14.5 million (before devaluation), based on head count, is made up by other sources of revenue, mainly dues and sponsorships.

As noted at the top of this Appendix, the most important conclusions in "Boys in a Box" are based on gross differences, which do not depend on precision. Hopefully, readers will be reassured that cited figures are, at minimum, reasonable, and, at best, close to reality.

The Author

Carlo Zezza's home is in Newton, Massachusetts. He is a member of the Cambridge Boat Club. After many years working in Europe, he retains a second home in France, where two sectional Carl Douglas singles are stored in the garage for himself and for Margarita, his wife.

Carlo's perceptions of rower development come from racing in both Europe and the USA.

As a data addict and from business experience, gathering facts to reach constructive conclusions is a reflex, expressed in "Boys in a Box".

Comments and criticism are equally welcome, directed to carlozezza2@gmail.com.

Made in the USA
San Bernardino, CA
24 March 2017